AF428206

LEGACY OF LOVE

A Handbook on Planning Your Funeral with Grace

Dr. Barbara A. Perkins, DMin., M.A., PCC

KP PUBLISHING COMPANY

ISBN: 979-8-994090-40-4 (Paperback)
ISBN: 979-8-994090-41-1 (eBook)

Library of Congress Control Number: Pending

Editor: Manuscript Mender
Cover Design & Photographer: Addis Huyler and Jason Rahming
Literary Director: Sandra Slayton James

Published by:

KP Publishing Company
Publisher of Fiction, Nonfiction, & Children's Books
Los Angeles ·Las Vegas
www.kp-pub.com
First Edition 2026

Printed in the United States of America

DEDICATION

To my family and those who will fulfill my wishes.

This family planning guide is my gift to you.

May my love for you be the example for your love for each other. May you find peace in knowing that I thought ahead and had Joy in remembering that I lived my life with gratitude and grace.

Let this be a guide for your heart as much as for your hands. May it help you design a homegoing celebration worthy of the life you have lived, and a lasting act of love for those who remain.

FOREWORD

When Barbara told me about *Legacy of Love*, I immediately recognized the depth of its purpose. For more than fifteen years, I have worked with families to plan, prepare, and organize their final arrangements.

I have witnessed time and again the difference between chaos and calm. In almost all cases, the difference comes down to *preparation*.

Losing a loved one is something no one ever wishes to happen. However, unfortunately, it is one of life's certainties. Apart from grieving and accommodating family and friends who want to pay their last respects, there are so many preparations to make just for the funeral service. Funerals bring people together, providing an opportunity to offer one another support and comfort during a painful time.

This book fills a space that has long been empty. Most people avoid thinking about their own funeral, not because they do not care, but because they do not know where to begin. Dr. Perkins approaches this subject with a gentleness and grace that make it not only approachable but also empowering.

In *Legacy of Love*, she bridges the practical and the spiritual, reminding us that planning one's funeral is not a morbid act, but a meaningful expression of love and responsibility. Her words and sensitivity will encourage readers to find peace in preparation and purpose.

In my experience as a specialist, I have witnessed how much comfort families feel when their loved ones have already made clear, thoughtful decisions. This guide will help every reader do just that: leave clarity instead of questions, calm instead of conflict, and celebration instead of confusion and remorse.

Dr. Perkins' wisdom, personal experience, compassion, and faith are the foundations of this book. *Legacy of Love* will help you plan your homegoing and guide you with grace.

Debra C. Thompson
Funeral & Cemetery Preplanning Specialist

PREFACE

When Preparation Becomes Love

I have learned over time that the truest form of love is preparation, not the kind born from fear, but from wisdom. When we prepare, we create ease for others. We take confusion off the shoulders of those who will already be carrying the weight of loss.

This handbook began as a simple desire to give my family, and all families, a way to plan for their own celebration of life with both clarity and grace. What I found in writing it was peace, the kind that comes when order replaces anxiety and intention replaces avoidance.

My hope is that *Legacy of Love* will inspire you to do the same, to face this sacred work not as something dark, but as something deeply healing. Preparing for your homegoing is not about dying; it is about ensuring that your final act on earth mirrors how you lived, with dignity, care, and love.

As you turn these pages, you may find courage, lightness, and yes, even joy in the process.

A life remembered in grace!

AUTHOR'S NOTE

I wrote *Legacy of Love: A Handbook on Planning Your Funeral with Grace* as both a guide and a reflective way to bring order and beauty to a subject we too often avoid. I have seen firsthand and experienced the uncertainty and pain that arise when families are forced to guess their loved one's wishes. I have witnessed the sense of calm that arises when things are written clearly, thoughtfully organized, and done with care.

This handbook is my way of teaching and coaching even in my absence. It gathers wisdom from faith, culture, and experience to make what can be difficult feel doable, and what feels heavy becomes light.

To my readers, may you find courage to prepare now, and comfort in knowing that preparation itself is a prayer. To my family, may these words remind you that I have loved you beyond measure. And when the time comes, may you celebrate me with laughter, beauty, and faith.

Legacy of Love is not a book about endings. It is a book about gratitude, legacy, and the eternal language of love.

Dr. Barbara A. Perkins

INTRODUCTION

Legacy of Love: A Handbook for Planning Your Funeral with Grace

There comes a time in every life when love must take on a new form, one that speaks when we no longer can. This book was born from that understanding: that preparing for our final celebration is not an act of fear, but one of devotion. It is love, thoughtfully arranged.

In Black American and Caribbean traditions, a funeral, often called a *homegoing*, is far more than a ceremony of farewell. It is a sacred reflection of how we lived, how we believed, and how we loved. It carries our music, our color, our stories, and our spirit. For generations, our people have said goodbye not in silence, but in song, in beauty, in faith, and often out loud.

I want my homegoing to reflect the life I have lived: joyful, elegant, grounded in faith, and filled with gratitude. I want the program, the music, the flowers, and even my final words to embody dignity, class, and grace. I want those who gather to feel lifted, to laugh through their tears, and to remember that I tried every day to encourage others and to live with intentionality and purpose.

Planning ahead is a gift of peace. It spares loved ones from the weight of uncertainty during their most tender hours. It allows them to rest in the comfort of knowing that every detail was chosen with care. My prayer is that this handbook helps others do the same, to plan with love, to prepare with clarity, and to celebrate with joy.

Table of Contents

*The final act of kindness is an offering
of love, entrusted to God, given in peace,
and remembered with grace.*

CHAPTER 1

A Final Act of Kindness

There is no greater act of kindness than preparing for the peace of those we will one day leave behind. Planning one's homegoing is not a fearful thing; it is a gesture of deep love and foresight. It is love, made practical and essential.

Why Planning Ahead Is Love in Action

I have witnessed how death can test even the strongest families. When my mother made her transition, our family of ten siblings was suddenly faced with the question: *How do we honor her?* Ten hearts, ten opinions, ten memories. What should have been a time of unity became a time of quiet disagreements and unspoken expectations. The pain of grief was compounded by secret confusion, guilt, and regrets. Over time, those small cracks grew wider, adding permanent distance between a once-close family. This distance demonstrated through silence over months and years continued to grow, especially after we lost three of our brothers, birthing imaginary stories and doubt cast on those simply trying to maintain respect and dignity. For me, some of the moments were more painful than the loss of our loved ones.

No family deserves that kind of division during a season of mourning. Planning spares those we love from uncertainty. It ensures that, even in our absence, our voice remains, gently guiding one of the most important processes with care. It is saying, *"Here is what I want, and I've already prepared the way."* That simple act keeps hearts together when emotions are most fragile. It would be difficult to dispute or disagree with a plan you have made for yourself.

The Peace It Gives Families

There is indescribable peace in knowing that your family will not have to guess. Every detail, from the tone of the service to the flowers, the music, the attire, becomes a love letter to those who remain. When your wishes are clearly expressed, your loved ones can grieve without confusion and celebrate without regret. I know this is not what most of us are taught or shown to do, but what if we all made this a priority in our families?

This planning gives families permission to focus on love rather than logistics. It says to them: *"You have done enough. Rest. Rejoice. Remember."*

A Celebration of Joy and Grace

I have always believed that the joy that carried me through life should also carry me home. I want my homegoing to be filled with the same laughter, beauty, and gratitude that defined my life. Regardless of status or means, everyone deserves a celebration that feels like *them.* Affordable options exist for every family.

The important thing is to take ownership right now, to leave both the plan and the resources to carry it out. That is what I call *the final act of love.* It is not about control; it is about care. You are gifting your family peace, direction, and the blessing of honoring your life exactly as you wished.

Chapter 1 Reflections: A Final Act of Kindness

Before you turn the page, I invite you to pause for just a moment.

You are not being asked to make decisions yet. There is no checklist to complete and nothing to finalize. It is simply an opportunity to notice what rises in you when you imagine your own homegoing, the feelings, the hopes, the hesitations, the quiet wishes that may already live in your heart.

Take a breath. Let your thoughts come without judgment.

Consider these questions and write whatever comes to mind. These first impressions are not permanent answers; they are simply a starting place. When you return to them after reading this book, you may be surprised by how your clarity has grown.

Reflect and write:

- When you imagine your funeral or homegoing, what feeling do you hope fills the room?

- Do you picture something quiet and intimate, or joyful and celebratory?

- What do you want your loved ones to experience that day, comfort, peace, gratitude, laughter, unity?

- Are there traditions, music, colors, or symbols that already feel meaningful to you?

- What worries you most about leaving these decisions to others?

- What would it mean to you to know that your family will not have to guess?

- In what ways could planning be an act of love rather than something to fear?

Write freely. There are no right or wrong answers here.

These early thoughts are the beginning of your legacy in words. As you move through the pages ahead, you will be given tools, language, and clarity to shape them into something lasting, a plan that brings peace to those you love and reflects the life you have lived with intention and grace.

*A funeral is a sacred gathering
where tears are welcomed, memories are
shared, and God meets us in our sorrow.*

CHAPTER 2

Understanding Funerals

Funerals are among the oldest human rituals. It is how we mark the transition from earthly life to eternal rest. In African, Black, and Caribbean traditions, these moments are layered with reverence, beauty, and meaning. Whether grand or humble, they are a collective act of honor, saying not just *farewell*, but *thank you for the life you lived.*

Different Types of Services

Every culture and family expresses grief and remembrance differently. The following are the most common types of services today:

- **Traditional Funeral Service:**

  Usually held in a church or funeral home, this service includes a viewing, religious or spiritual ceremony, and burial. It follows long-held customs, often centered around faith and family unity. The most popular type includes an in-ground burial.

- **Memorial Service:**

  Takes place after a burial or cremation, focusing on memories rather than the presence of the body. This service often invites storytelling and reflection, allowing time to celebrate a life lived.

- **Celebration of Life:**

  A more modern approach that is often informal, colorful, and joyful. Instead of mourning, the tone is gratitude. Attendees may wear bright colors, share laughter, and focus on moments of triumph and joy.

- **Cremation Ceremony:**

  Simpler in structure, often followed by scattering of ashes or placement in a memorial site. Families may combine this with a separate memorial service. This type has been rapidly becoming more popular since 2022, the COVID-19 era.

- **Green or Eco-Friendly Burial:**

  A returns to simplicity, often without chemicals, metal caskets, or vaults. The body is returned to the earth naturally, a fitting choice for those who wish to live and depart gently on the planet.

- **Repast:**

  A communal meal after the service, where laughter and tears meet. The repast, especially in Black families, is where healing begins. Food becomes ministry, and shared stories soften the ache of goodbye.

The Caribbean Processional: A Parade of Reverence

Growing up in the Bahamas, then a British Colony, funerals were formal and public occasions. They were meant for an entire community to pause and pay their respects. The day would begin with lines of cars, mostly black, their headlights glowing under the island sun. However, the lines of people prepared to walk were usually much longer. They moved slowly through the streets, following the hearse in solemn procession.

For those watching, it felt like a holiday parade, but of reverence. People would stand still as the motorcade passed, men removing their hats, women lowering their heads. It was a sight to behold: a people united in respect, mourning as one body. Even young children like me have learned the importance of respecting the dead, whether you knew them personally or not. We knew they belonged to a family grieving for a loved one.

In many communities, the final leg of the journey was done on foot. Family members and close friends would follow the casket to the cemetery, singing hymns or led by brass bands and drumbeats. The rhythm of the drums, the weight of the silence, the grace of the march, it was both sorrow and celebration intertwined. That processional taught me early in life that funerals are not about death alone. They are about belonging, honor, and community love.

The Evolution of the Black Homegoing Tradition

Across the Americas, the Black homegoing grew out of faith and survival. For enslaved Africans, death was not merely an ending; it was liberation, a return to the ancestors, a journey home. This belief birthed the concept of the "homegoing," a spiritual crossing over into eternal freedom.

Over time, the Black church became the center of these ceremonies. The preacher would declare, "Weeping may endure for a night, but joy cometh in the morning." Choirs would sing with power, the congregation would shout "Amen," and the service would become a testimony and celebration of triumph over death.

Cultural and Spiritual Meaning Behind Rituals

From the Caribbean to the American South, beauty and formality are integral to our farewells. Attendees dress in their best, black suits and hats, crisp white gloves, fine lace, or African attire rich with color and symbolism. Frequently, the deceased's close family members would wear matching, preselected fabrics designed to their liking. The service might include scripture, spirituals, and tributes, often followed by laughter at the repast, where memories soften the ache of loss. Programs are carefully planned and thought out.

Every gesture, from the handkerchief waved in goodbye to the songs sung, the placing of the flowers or special objects, and salutes at the graveside, carries the same message: *this life matters.*

Today, homegoing's remain vibrant expressions of culture, faith, and identity. Whether in a grand cathedral or a small community church, the spirit is the same: *We honor life, we rejoice in the spirit, and we give thanks for the journey.*

The Many Ways We Say Goodbye

While every funeral shares a purpose to honor a life, the style and tone vary across traditions, faiths, and social standing. In planning your own funeral, you get to choose, and your family is relieved from the stress of trying to get it just right. This gift is truly one that sets the bar high.

Traditional African Funerals and Their Pageantry

Across Africa, funerals are not mere farewells; they are sacred homegoing's. Rooted in the belief that death is a passage to ancestral life, these ceremonies are among the most elaborate social events, often lasting several days and uniting entire communities.

The pageantry begins with music, drumming, and dance, living expressions of love and respect. Attendees wear traditional attire in symbolic colors: black and red for mourning in Ghana, white for a long, blessed life in parts of Nigeria. Processions are vibrant and public, with singers, praise poets, and family members escorting the casket amid song and prayer.

Each element carries a spiritual purpose: to honor the life lived and to guide the spirit peacefully to the ancestors. After the burial, the community gathers for feasting and dancing, transforming grief into gratitude.

In every rhythm, chant, and tear, a truth endures that life continues through memory, community, and the beauty of the send-off. Traditional African funerals remind us that to celebrate the departed is to keep their spirit alive.

Royal Funerals

Royal funerals represent the height of ceremonial tradition. Every detail, from the tolling bells to the processional route, is steeped in centuries of symbolism. They are public declarations of history, heritage, and continuity. Precision, reverence, and pageantry remind us that a life can be celebrated with both grandeur and grace, lessons that can be adapted to any farewell, no matter how intimate. The most-watched Royal Funeral of our time was that of Queen Elizabeth II and Princess Diana in 1997.

State or Dignitary Funerals

These honors individuals who served with distinction, heads of state, national heroes, or faith leaders. They include military escorts, official tributes, and moments of collective silence. The service for Dr. Martin Luther King Jr. remains one of the most powerful examples: a blending of activism, worship, and reverence for a life given to service.

Funerals for U.S. presidents and national leaders are among the most solemn ceremonies in the country, reflecting both personal legacy and public service. State Funerals follow precise traditions of honor and reverence.

The casket, draped in the American flag, often lies in state in the U.S. Capitol Rotunda for citizens to pay their respects. A military honor guard keeps constant vigil, and the procession that follows may include a riderless horse and a 21-gun salute, the nation's highest tribute.

Services are usually held in the National Cathedral or a home church, blending hymns, scripture, and personal eulogies with formal tributes from government and world leaders.

The burial that follows is often simple yet deeply symbolic, marking the end of an era and the continuation of the ideals the leader stood for. These funerals remind the nation that while leadership ends, service and sacrifice remain part of the country's enduring story.

High-Profile Funerals

High-profile funerals celebrate public figures whose influence crossed boundaries, such as artists, community icons, or entrepreneurs. They often feature live music, public tributes, and media coverage, offering the world a chance to mourn collectively. Aretha Franklin's homegoing held in Detroit in 2018, for example, was both regal and joyful, a concert of faith, love, and legacy, which turned into a powerful expression of Black culture, spirituality, and gratitude for her legacy. Others, such as Michael Jackson's in 2009, held at the Staples Center in Los Angeles, drew millions of viewers worldwide, blending grief with celebration as well as global culture.

In contrast, Whitney Houston's funeral in 2012 took place in New Hope Baptist Church, where she sang as a child. The service was intimate yet globally broadcast, filled with beautiful music and prayers.

Military Funerals

These ceremonies reflect discipline and devotion. With flags, honor guards, and the haunting melody of "Taps," they honor the courage and service of those who defended their country. Even if one never wore a uniform, this level of dignity can inspire how we honor lives devoted to service in any form.

Religious and Cultural Funerals

Every faith expresses grief uniquely.

- Christians gather in worship and song.

- Jews sit in *shiva*, surrounded by love and prayer.

- Muslims bury swiftly, in simplicity, and surrender to God's will.

- Hindus cremate, chanting prayers that release the spirit.

- Africans and Afro-Caribbeans celebrate through drumming, dancing, and storytelling, proof that even in mourning, joy is sacred.

Destination and Themed Funerals

Modern times have given rise to more personal farewells, on beaches, in gardens, or at family homes. This year, a friend of mine planned and hosted fifty guests for the Celebration of Life for her beloved Mother-in-Law. It was in their backyard, where the view and smell of the flowers from the nursery behind their home were the most aesthetically pleasing.

Themed funerals might reflect a person's passions: a teacher's service in a school auditorium, a gardener's farewell among flowers, a musician's life remembered through song. These designs remind us that goodbye can be beautiful when it tells the truth of who we were.

Reflection

Whether quiet or grand, sacred, or simple, every farewell tells a story. The real power of a funeral lies not in its scale, but in its sincerity.

From the Caribbean processional to a royal cortege, from the church pews to the graveside drumbeat, the purpose is the same: to affirm that a life was lived with meaning, that love endures beyond the body, and that remembrance keeps the spirit alive.

"The question is not how large the ceremony should be, but how truthfully it reflects the soul it honors." Dr. Barbara A. Perkins

Chapter 2 Reflection: Understanding Funerals

Take a few moments to reflect. Write freely. These are not final decisions, only early thoughts, and impressions. What resonates with you in chapter 2?

- As you read about the many ways we say goodbye, which traditions or ceremonies stirred something in you?

- When you imagine your own farewell, do you feel drawn more toward something quiet and intimate or public and communal?

- Which elements feel essential to your story, faith, music, culture, pageantry, simplicity, or community gathering?

- How important is it to you that your funeral reflects your ancestry, cultural identity, or spiritual roots? What would you want others to see or feel about who you are and where you come from?

- What role do you want your community to play in your farewell? Who do you imagine standing with your family, walking with them, remembering with them?

- Are there any funerals you have attended, traditional, celebratory, high-profile, or intimate, that left a lasting impression on you?

- How do you want your life to be described through the way you are honored, humble, joyful, faithful, dignified, service-driven, or all of the above?

Each life is God's unique creation, and every farewell should reflect the story He authored.

CHAPTER 3

Designing a Celebration That Reflects You

Your homegoing should feel like looking in a mirror, one last reflection of your spirit, your story, and your style. It is not vanity; it is legacy. It is a legacy because it continues your influence beyond your lifetime, guiding how others remember and celebrate you. By leaving clear instructions and heartfelt intentions, you model love, order, and foresight. Values that your family can carry forward in their own lives.

Setting the Tone and Theme

My ideal celebration would feel like a *Spiritual Joy Fest,* filled with light, laughter, music, and gratitude. I would want it to feel more like a gathering than a goodbye. I want people to arrive dressed for a grand celebration, elegant, polished, culturally beautiful. This is not a day for sadness, but for testimony and witness.

My chosen colors will be white, representing peace and divine transition, with bold accents of deep red. Red, for me, symbolizes love, vitality, and my enduring connection to my beloved sisterhood, *Delta Sigma Theta Sorority, Inc.* It will also honor the powerful lineage of women who taught me to lead with grace and serve with purpose.

What tone would you like to set for your final goodbye? Have you ever thought about it? I am excited for you and encourage you to step into this process with enthusiasm. Like the feeling you get when you are shopping for a special someone for a special occasion.

Elegance, Class, and Afrocentric Beauty

Classy are not about cost; it is about care. I envision an atmosphere of dignity and refinement with roses everywhere, red, and lush, with touches of African design elements that honor my heritage. An Afrocentric influence might show through fabrics, head wraps, or wearable art, all reminders that we are people of majesty and resilience. The red carpet, of course, is to demonstrate what I feel about every guest. I would want each guest to feel as special as I do when I enter any event with a dedicated red carpet. Guests should walk in and *feel* my spirit, beauty in every corner, love in every detail.

Music and Spirit

Music has always been my language of worship and joy. I imagine the sounds of CeCe Winans, Tasha Cobbs Leonard, Yolanda Adams, Kirk Franklin, and others filling the air, powerful, uplifting voices declaring victory and faith. The music should rise like sunlight, reminding everyone that I have simply gone home to my final resting place. Some of the most popular funeral songs and favorites of mine are: "Wind Beneath My Wings", "My Heart Will Go On", "I Hope You Dance", "One Sweet Day", "Mama's Song", "My Way, Take Me To The King", "Because You Love Me", "The Lord's Prayer, Time To Say Goodbye", "Tears In Heaven and Hero", to name a few. Do you have a play list for your family to consider?

Personal Touches and Keepsakes

Photographs tell the story no words can. I plan to spend time selecting high-quality photos from throughout my life, childhood, motherhood, travels, milestones, and to create a keepsake book that captures the fullness of my time on earth. These images will speak when I cannot, showing the laughter, love, and lessons that shaped me. For the past seven years, I have ordered my past year's books through Facebook. It consists of all the photos I posted. This is one way to begin collecting photos.

Guests will receive a beautifully designed program and a keepsake booklet filled with those photos, something to hold, to remember, and to smile over. Remember, it is a part of your legacy and the way you wish to be remembered with joy.

Perhaps there will also be a "Memory Lane" gallery, temporarily installed, where people can walk among moments, each photo a whisper: *She lived fully. She loved it deeply.*

Your funeral is not just a ceremony. It is the final signature of your soul, the ultimate reflection of who you were, and how you want to be remembered.

Chapter 3 Reflection: Designing a Celebration That Reflects You

Take another deep breath before you begin writing your reflections. Remember this is not about perfection, it is about authenticity. Write freely and without editing yourself. These reflections will evolve as you continue reading.

- When you imagine your homegoing, what do you want the atmosphere to feel like the moment people enter?

- Would you prefer your farewell to feel more like a gathering, a celebration, or a sacred service?

- What words best describe the tone you envision? (Joyful, peaceful, elegant, reverent, celebratory, intimate, vibrant.)

- How important is elegance or formality to you? What does "class and dignity" mean in your own language?

- Are there colors that carry meaning for you? What emotions or memories do those colors represent?

- What role should music play in your celebration, background, centerpiece, worship, storytelling, or joy-filled remembrance?

- Are there specific songs, artists, or styles of music that feel like the soundtrack of your life?

- What visual elements matter most to you, flowers, fabrics, lighting, photographs, symbols, or personal objects?

CHAPTER 4

Faith, Music, and Message

Faith: Declaring What You Believe

Your faith is your compass, the unseen hand that has guided your life and will now guide your transition into your next beautiful life. Stating what you believe gives your family a sacred framework for celebrating you. It roots your homegoing in meaning and memory.

As for me, I am a Christian woman who believes in God the Father, the Son, and the Holy Spirit as one divine presence expressed in power, grace, and love. I also draw deeply from my Caribbean ancestry, where the prayers of my ancestors still whisper through time. Their faith and rituals, songs at dawn, prayers over food, anointing the sick, and lighting candles in remembrance of others are, to me, sacred expressions of continuity with God, the Supreme Being. Those ancestral practices still protect, comfort, and intercede on my behalf. Therefore, I lift them up and offer many of the same rituals in my daily life.

At my homegoing, I would want those who attend to feel both my Christian devotion and my ancestral pride. My faith honors both scripture and spirit. Prayer, scripture reading, and the acknowledgment of the ancestors' presence should be welcomed, but within the reverence of Christian worship and practices.

Each person should define this for themselves:

- What is the faith or belief system that shaped your life?

- What spiritual practices kept you grounded?

- How should they be reflected in your farewell?

For some, it involves a church service with communion; for others, pouring libations for ancestors. For many, both reflect the belief that love and spirit endure.

Music: The Soundtrack of Your Spirit

Music has the power to speak when words fall short. It soothes, uplifts, and gathers people in unity. For centuries, in Black life and worship, music has been our language of faith and resistance, the way we remind the world that even in loss, we sing. An experience that amplifies this truth in recent years is watching how music and singing have become a constant in my husband's life as we live through his diagnosis of dementia. Music takes him back to good memories and keeps him calm and joyful as he creates new memories.

Consider what role you want music to play in your homegoing. Do you want an atmosphere of sacred stillness or one of high praise and rejoicing? Would you prefer spirituals, gospel, hymns, or soft instrumentals? Music sets the emotional temperature of your farewell.

For my celebration, I would want it filled with uplifting, soul-stirring gospel music that feels alive. Let there be CeCe Winans, Tasha Cobbs Leonard, Kirk Franklin, or

Richard Smallwood, voices that move the spirit and lift the heart. Let the choir sing as if the heavens are opening. I would want every note to remind those in attendance that joy is still possible and that my story ended in peace.

In planning your music:

- Choose songs that capture your faith journey.

- Balance sacred and celebratory tones.

- Consider instrumental interludes for reflection.

- Assign songs purposefully: one to open, one to comfort, one to uplift.

Music should guide your guests through your story, the quiet of prayer, the rise of praise, and the gentle closure with peace.

Message: The Words That Remain

Every homegoing carries a message, not just about how a person died, but how they lived. The message is the final voice of your life's purpose. You can decide now what you want it to say.

Traditionally, families leave this part to a pastor or officiant, trusting them to deliver a eulogy that comforts and inspires. That may still be your choice, but you can also shape the tone and content in advance.

Ask yourself:

- What do I want people to remember about my life?

- What do I want them to take away from my faith, love, and legacy?

- Who do I trust to speak with both strength and serenity?

Choose someone who can deliver your message without breaking under the weight of emotion, perhaps a minister who knows you well, a spiritual friend, or a trusted mentee. You may still invite family members to share short reflections, but the main message should be anchored in calm assurance and knowledge of you and your beliefs.

For my homegoing, I would want the message to echo themes of gratitude, service, and joy, that life, even with its trials, was worth living fully. I would want the speaker, my minister of the church I hold membership in, to talk about the grace that covered me, shaped me, and carried me. I would want the room to feel light when they leave, as though hope itself spoke. We do not know the time we will die or who will be here after we are gone. However, we can write a plan that includes the people you know today who would honor the role of speaking at your homegoing celebration. In my life, I have been blessed to know a few who could and would speak for me in this way: Dr. Iyanla Vanzant, Dr. Barbara Williams-Skinner, Dr. Michael Eric Dyson, Dr. Paul Thibodeaux, Minister Tammilee Jules, and Dr. Shavon Arline-Bradley. My family will not have a problem with identifying the right people to participate in this celebration.

Reflection Prompt for the Reader:

- Write your faith statement: *What do you believe?*

- List the songs or artists that represent your spiritual journey.

- Decide now who will deliver your message and what they should bring to it.

Chapter 4 Reflection: Faith, Music, and Message

Before you write, pause and center yourself. This chapter is about meaning what you believe, what you hope, and what you want your life to say in the end.

Reflect honestly and gently.

- How would you describe your faith or spiritual foundation in your own words?

- What beliefs have carried you through life's most joyful moments and its most difficult seasons?

- Are there specific scriptures, prayers, poems, or sacred readings that have sustained you? Why do they matter to you?

- What role should music play in expressing your faith, joy, or testimony?

- Do you imagine sacred hymns, contemporary worship, spirituals, gospel, instrumental music, or a blend that reflects your journey?

- Are there songs that feel like your personal testimony, moments when music helped you survive, heal, or rejoice?

- When someone speaks at your service, what tone do you hope they carry, celebratory, reflective, comforting, hopeful, or instructive?

- Would you prefer prepared remarks from selected speakers, or spontaneous reflections? Why?

- If your homegoing could deliver one final message to those gathered, what would you want them to hear and remember?

Preparation is love in action; a quiet prayer answered before it is ever spoken.

CHAPTER 5

Preparing Practically

Faith gives peace to the heart, but planning gives rest to the mind. When your affairs are in order, your family can grieve in grace rather than confusion. Preparation is love in motion, that final gift of clarity. This chapter provides a practical checklist or roadmap for planning your own funeral. These details you record now spare your loved ones from the stress of it later. Like me, you may have had an unfavorable opinion of someone who planned their own funeral in the past.

The idea of planning one's own funeral felt unsettling, even inappropriate. It was something rare and whispered about as something morbid, unnecessary, or prideful. The common thought was that the person was trying to control life from beyond the grave or draw attention to themselves. Families preferred to leave such matters unspoken, trusting that "someone would handle it" when the time came. But times have changed.

Today, we understand that planning our own farewell is not an act of vanity, but of compassion. It is a clear, loving gesture that eases emotional and financial burdens for those we leave behind. In a world more aware of the importance of mental, emotional, and spiritual preparedness, this kind of planning has become a mark of wisdom and care, a way to say, *I lived intentionally, and I will depart the same way.*

The Legacy of Love Practical Checklist

This list is an exhaustive guide divided into seven sections. Take what works for you and leave the rest for others to consider as options for their planning.

1. Funeral and Service Arrangements

- Choose and document your preferred funeral home or mortuary.

- Decide on your service type: traditional, memorial, homegoing, or celebration of life.

- Identify the location: church, chapel, special venue, or destination.

- Select officiant(s) or clergy to lead the service.

- Choose readers, speakers, and musicians.

- Determine whether you prefer burial, cremation, or an alternative service.

- If burial: identify cemetery, plot location, and title/deed information.

- Select casket or urn preference (style, color, materials). Purchase in advance if possible.

- Decide on flowers, photography, videography, or live streaming.

- Decide on details for the repast: location, catering, and attendees.

2. Legal and Administrative Documents

- Last Will and Testament should be reviewed and updated regularly to keep it current.

- Revocable Living Trust, with listed beneficiaries.

- Power of Attorney and Health Care Directive filed and shared with the executor.

- Birth certificate, Social Security card, and photo ID stored in one location.

- Marriage certificates, divorce decrees, and military discharge papers.

- Deeds or property titles for real estate or vehicles.

- Digital copies stored securely (USB drive, encrypted file, or trusted cloud folder).

- Executor or trustee contact information clearly listed.

- All passwords and mailing lists of close friends and family.

3. Financial, Insurance, and Prepaid Services

- Review and update life insurance policies with the correct beneficiaries.

- Note all bank accounts, credit unions, and investments.

- Document retirement accounts, pensions, and annuities.

- Record loan and mortgage details with account numbers.

- Keep receipts or contracts for prepaid funeral or burial services.

- List contact information for your financial advisor, CPA, or attorney.

- Leave instructions for settling membership dues, credit cards, or online subscriptions.

- Organizations and charities' instructions and dues.

4. Obituary and Program Preparation

- Draft your personal obituary, or provide notes on tone, highlights, and key milestones.

- Select one or two high-quality photos for use in printed or digital materials.

- Leave samples of how you wish your program to be laid out and what to include.

- Leave contact information for preferred vendors, if available to you.

- Include scriptures, quotes, or poetry to be printed in the program.

- Provide a list of honorary pallbearers, ushers, or family representatives.

- Specify if you prefer flowers, charitable donations, or acts of service in lieu of gifts.

5. Communication and Connections

- Emergency contacts: family, friends, faith leaders, and executors.

- List of organizations or memberships:

  - Sororities/fraternities

  - Church or ministry affiliations

  - Community or service organizations

  - Professional boards and associations

  - Neighborhood Association Contact.

- Social Media Accounts and Online Presence:

    o Facebook, Instagram, LinkedIn, Twitter/X, TikTok, YouTube

    o Email accounts and personal websites.

    o Include usernames and passwords (stored securely)

    o Indicate if you would like accounts memorialized or deleted.

- Mailing list or contacts for obituary notifications or announcements.

+

6. Costs and Budget Planning

- Obtain written estimates from your funeral home.

- In advance, one can purchase a funeral package that is all-inclusive.

- Include line items for:

    o Casket or urn.

    o Venue and service fees.

    o Flowers and décor.

    o Musicians, officiants, and program printing.

    o Photography, video, or streaming services.

    o Repast catering. Estimate attendance.

- Keep a copy of your funeral budget worksheet in your "Legacy of Love" folder. Specify where the funds needed would come from. (E.g., Insurance payout, money in the bank, or cash left on hand, and where to find it.)

7. Organizing and Storing Your Plan

- Create a **Legacy of Love Binder** or digital folder.

- Include all documents, lists, passwords, and contracts.

- Secure a fireproof docu-file, bag, or safe that is large enough to hold all things.

- Store in a fireproof safe or safe-deposit box.

- Give copies or access to your executive or next of kin.

- Review and update every one to two years or after major life events or birthdays.

Reflection

Preparation is a sacred act, the quiet organization of love. When you take these steps now, you make space for your family to grieve in peace and remember you with joy. Your order becomes their comfort; you are planning their release.

Chapter 5 Reflections: Preparing Practically

1. How prepared do you feel today regarding the practical details of your homegoing? What areas need your attention first?

2. Have you selected a funeral home or service provider you trust? If not, what qualities or values matter most to you in choosing one?

3. Do you have life insurance, pre-need arrangements, or a trust in place to cover funeral costs? What steps are needed to ensure your family will not face a financial burden?

4. Who should be responsible for carrying out your wishes? Are they aware of your preferences and prepared to follow them?

5. What legal documents (will, trust, power of attorney, Five Wishes) need to be created or updated?

6. Where will your important documents be stored, and who will know how to access them?

7. Have you written a contact list of family, friends, sorority sisters, church, and organizations that should be notified? Who should lead the communication?

8. What information do you want included or excluded in your obituary? Are you prepared to write or draft it yourself?

*Through spoken tributes
and shared memories, God allows love
to echo beyond this life.*

CHAPTER 6

Voices and Tributes

Every voice that rises at your homegoing becomes part of your legacy. The way someone speaks, what they communicate, and their style of delivery all influence how others will remember them.

There was a time when planning one's own funeral, down to who would speak, was viewed as unnecessary or even vain. People assumed that loved ones would "just know" what to say. But experience has shown how easily that good intention can go sideways. In moments of deep emotion, people speak from the heart but not always from discernment. Some tell jokes that are fine in private but not suitable for sacred settings. Others ramble in grief, bringing discomfort instead of comfort.

Every voice that rises at your homegoing becomes part of your legacy. That is why choosing the right people matters. Be intentional. Select those who can tell your story with clarity, affection, and composure. While it is common to hope that family members will speak, it is also worthwhile to consider inviting close friends, mentees, or respected community members who can share heartfelt and sincere messages while remaining composed. You are curating the closing chapter of your story, and giving it the dignity, tone, and grace your life deserves.

Choosing Who Will Speak

- Choose a lead officiant (pastor, minister, or faith leader).

- Identify two, three, or as many voices you wish to represent different chapters of your life, family, friend, mentor, mentee, and professional colleague.

- Keep tributes brief (2–3 minutes each) to maintain the flow of the service.

- Let one person coordinate all speakers for timing and tone. This can be an arduous task.

Writing Your Obituary or Personal Message

Writing your obituary can be one of the most personal and challenging parts of planning your homegoing. It requires looking at your life with honesty, humility, and gratitude. Revising it multiple times is expected. Each draft becomes a reflection, helping you see your life from a wider, gentler view.

Your obituary is not just an announcement of your passing; it is your final story, a celebration of the journey you have lived. It should include the essentials: your full name, birth and transition dates, family members, career highlights, and contributions. But beyond the facts, let it carry your warmth. Write about what you loved, how you served, and what mattered most to you. Share the lessons that shaped you and the values you hope your family will carry forward.

I chose to think of my obituary as a *draft,* not a fixed statement, but a starting point. I want those I leave behind to feel free to add their own reflections and memories, to make it something we share. This approach takes away the heaviness and invites collaboration, turning the obituary into a collective act of remembrance rather than a formal summary.

You may also include a personalized message and a short letter to your loved ones to be read aloud or printed in the program. It might express peace, blessings, or gratitude, reminding them that your love remains. Long after the music fades and the flowers are gone, those words will still speak comfort.

Legacy Letters for Loved Ones

Personal letters to family members can be the most heartfelt and the most challenging part of preparing your homegoing. There is so much to say, and sometimes it is hard to find the right words for each person who has meant something to you. You may want to say one thing to your children, something else to your spouse, and something different still to close friends or siblings. I chose to write both a collective letter that can be included in the funeral program and individual letters that will be read privately by each family member.

A legacy letter is your voice preserved, a love note that time cannot silence. It is your chance to say what life may not have given you time to express. Each letter might include:

- Words of affirmation and encouragement.

- Blessings for their future.

- A memory you cherish.

- A prayer or scripture chosen especially for them.

These letters are a sacred exchange between hearts. You can put them in sealed envelopes to give out after the service or keep them securely with your estate papers. Regardless of how you deliver them, these words aim to reassure your loved ones that your messages will continue to provide guidance, comfort, and support even in your absence.

Final Thought

Throughout my life, I have sought to leave every person I encounter with something lasting, a good feeling, a meaningful word, or a thought they can return to when they need it most. It is the same intention that guides this part of the journey. Should I never have the chance to speak again, I hope that my words, teachings, or inspiration will continue to make my presence felt.

Your tributes, your words, and your chosen voices are the echoes of your life. When you decide who speaks and what they share, you create a final gift, a message that carries comfort, wisdom, and peace. It is the same spirit I bring to my coaching: even if there is only one conversation, I want it to matter. Let your homegoing do the same. Let it sound exactly like you, thoughtful, strong, and full of grace.

Chapter 6 Reflection: Voices and Tributes

1. Who do you trust to speak about your life with clarity, love, and composure? Are there people you prefer not to speak publicly to at your service? Write your reasons gently and honestly.

2. What stories from your life would you want to highlight or remembered? If one person could express the essence of who you were, who would that be? What makes them the right choice?

3. Who should read your obituary? Someone steady? A loved one? A close friend?

4. Would you like your obituary to be fully written by you or co-written with someone you trust?

5. Which relationships in your life deserve special mention or acknowledgement?

6. What blessings, prayers, or affirmations do you want spoken over your family?

7. Who would you choose to represent different aspects of your life? (Family, faith, sorority, professional work, community.)

8. Is there someone whose voice would bring healing, unity, or peace to your family? Consider naming them.

48

*God speaks through every culture
and custom, reminding us that love
transcends how we say goodbye.*

CHAPTER 7

The Cultural Language of Goodbye

No one ever really wants to say goodbye. The word itself feels too final, too sharp for something as sacred as love. Yet saying goodbye, and how we do it, is one of the truest reflections of who we are. For people of African descent, both in America and across the Caribbean, the farewell is more than a ceremony; it is a tapestry woven from faith, ancestry, and beauty. Our way of parting speaks the cultural language of dignity, pride, and belonging. It is a language of music, movement, food, and color, where goodbye becomes an act of love rather than loss.

African American and Caribbean Customs

Our homegoing traditions have long carried the soul of our history, a blend of African spirituality, Christian faith, and ancestral reverence. In both African American and Caribbean communities, funerals are not quiet departures but communal expressions of gratitude. Tears fall beside laughter; grief rises with song. We weep, sing, and celebrate, knowing that death is not the end but a passage, a returning home.

Dust to Dust

In the end, every story returns to the same truth: *from dust we came, and to dust we shall return.* Those words are not about loss but about belonging. They remind us that life is sacred in every form, that our bodies return to the earth even as our spirits rise to God.

Dust to dust is not a phrase of despair; it is a benediction. Everything, love, work, or wisdom shared, has value and is never wasted. The earth receives what heaven first gave, and the cycle of creation continues unbroken.

When my time comes, I hope those who gather will hear those words and feel peace. I pray they will understand that my story, like every life well lived, is simply changing form, from breath to memory, from presence to legacy, from dust to dust, and love to light.

I learned this deeply at the beginning of the COVID-19 pandemic when my maternal grandmother, who was ninety-eight, passed away in a nursing home. Once vibrant and funny, her voice had grown quieter in those final months. As we faced the restrictions of isolation and fear, I could not bear for her story to end as a "COVID death." I wished her legacy, a lifetime of faith, laughter, and love, to be defined by how she lived, not how she died. We had hoped she would reach one hundred, but I found peace in letting go of that wish. What mattered was that her goodbye felt whole, filled with gratitude and memory rather than fear.

There are also times when we want suffering to end. My beloved friend, Lois Buckman, fought a hard and unequal battle with cancer, one that was not fair and brought far too much pain. In those moments, our prayer changes. The goodbye we resist becomes mercy, a release. Even then, our cultural and spiritual traditions help us find meaning, reminding us that love can outlive pain.

The Unspoken Language of Our Culture

In Black culture, there is a whole layer of communication that lives beyond words, a shared rhythm of glances, sounds, and gestures that only those within the tribe understand. It is the quiet language of belonging, passed down through generations, often without formal teaching.

A single raised eyebrow can mean *"Don't start."* A long blink might say, *"I hear you, but I'm done with this conversation."* A soft sigh, a side-eye, or the sharp click of the tongue, all of these carry volumes of meaning. In church, a hum or a low *"Mmm-hmm"* can affirm a truth before the preacher even finishes the sentence. A hand laid gently on the shoulder says, *"I've got you."* A shared look across the room between elders can redirect a whole situation without a word spoken.

These nuances are part of what makes our gatherings, even funerals, feel sacred and communal. The nods, the knowing smiles, the call-and-response murmurs of *"Yes, Lord"* or *"Take your time"* are not interruptions; they are affirmations, ways of holding one another in sound and spirit.

In this unspoken language, we find comfort, humor, and respect. It conveys a sense of kinship, demonstrating that we are seen, understood, and connected, even in silence.

Food, Dress, Music, and Symbols That Carry Meaning

Our farewells are sensory; they look, sound, and taste like us.

- **Food** connects the living. The smell of collard greens, peas, and rice, or baked macaroni, fills the air, feeding both body and spirit. These shared meals are acts of comfort and communion, where grief softens in the warmth of community.

- **Dress** reflects reverence. Whether in traditional black and white, head wraps, or Sunday-best attire, we come dressed in honor. In many Caribbean settings, guests wear bright garments with hope and pride, because to us, every life is royal.

- **Music** lifts sorrow into praise. From church choirs and gospel hymns to steel pans and African drums, rhythm becomes prayer. The songs we sing and the music we play remind us that life and spirit continue, that joy and remembrance can coexist.

- **Symbols** such as flowers, candles, fans, and T-shirts with messages. Libations bridge heaven and earth. They symbolize light, presence, and the link between the living and those who have passed.

How These Reflect Ancestry and Pride

These customs are not mere rituals; they are affirmations of who we are and whose we are. They remind us that even in grief, we are people who choose beauty, community, and strength. Each song sung, each handheld, and each dish shared reflects our lineage, a people who have turned sorrow into ceremony for generations.

Our language of goodbye carries ancestral pride. It says: *We remember. We honor. We continue.* Whether standing at a graveside or gathered in a church pew, our goodbyes echo with faith and gratitude. They transform endings into celebrations, not because the pain is not real, but because love is stronger still.

Goodbye, in our culture, is never the end of the story. It is the beginning of remembering well.

Chapter 7 Reflection: The Cultural Language of Goodbye

1. What cultural traditions from your family or community bring you comfort during times of loss? Which of these would you want included in your homegoing?

2. How has your upbringing, whether Southern, Caribbean, African American, or otherwise, shaped your understanding of funerals and celebration of life services?

3. Are there rituals, songs, or symbols from your cultural heritage that feel essential to your farewell? (Examples: processionals, specific hymns, attire, colors, readings.)

4. What family stories or ancestral practices do you want honored or acknowledged at your service?

5. Are there foods or communal traditions that represent your heritage? Would you like these included at the repast?

6. Are there specific garments, fabrics, colors, or adornments that reflect your cultural identity? (African prints, Caribbean whites, Delta red and white, etc.)

*A life anchored in God leaves
behind peace, not confusion, not fear,
but rest for those who remain.*

CHAPTER 8

Leaving a Legacy of Peace

Leaving a legacy of peace is more than material inheritance; it is about the emotional and spiritual order we leave behind. It is giving the gift of clarity to those who love us so that they can move forward without confusion or conflict. Peace becomes the final blessing, the quiet harmony that continues long after we are gone.

What It Means to Leave Clarity and Order

I have witnessed in my own large family how easily our perceptions of relationships can differ from reality. The way we remember our closeness, our trust, or even our shared history may not match how others experienced it. You may believe your bond with a family member was solidly rooted in love and confidentiality, only to discover after their passing that things were not as they seemed.

I have lived this truth. Three of my six younger brothers have died, and with each loss, unexpected stories surfaced, stories that had to be communicated, translated, and gently unpacked to soothe hurt feelings and calm confusion. The fallout from those revelations lingered. It required patience, forgiveness, and deep spiritual work to move through the pain and begin repairing what was broken.

Death not only ends a life; it stirs everything beneath the surface. It can expose hidden tensions and unspoken truths. But acknowledging this reality is part of leaving a legacy of peace, understanding that healing begins with honesty, and that sometimes, clarity comes only through courage and compassion.

The Healing Power of Knowing Your Loved One's Wishes

There is comfort in knowing that a loved one's plans are already made. It removes doubt and prevents regret. When a family can say, *"She told us exactly what she wanted,"* it transforms grief into gratitude.

However, in large families or complex dynamics, these plans can also reveal long-buried feelings. Sometimes, clarity is misread as control. There may be assumptions that one sibling or relative had "too much influence" or that your decisions were made unfairly. It is not uncommon, especially in families where birth order or age determines an unspoken hierarchy.

I have seen it happen many times. In one family, the eldest sibling assumed she would naturally make all decisions, but her mother had chosen a younger daughter, the one most organized, to handle the estate and funeral arrangements. At first, it caused tension. But when the family gathered and read their mother's written instructions in her own handwriting, warm, firm, and full of love, peace settled in the room. What had started as suspicion turned into relief. Her clarity removed doubt, and her voice, even in absence, restored order.

Another example: a man left detailed instructions about his memorial service, down to the music and readers, but did not share his reasoning. His children felt left out and hurt. When families are not prepared for the details, even well-intentioned plans can spark misunderstanding. That is why communication is key; sharing your "why" matters just as much as sharing your "what."

Encouraging Others to Do the Same

Once you have made your plans, invite your family into the conversation. Do it gently, at the right time, with love. Explain your choices and how they reflect your values, not favoritism, but forethought. Let them know your decisions come from a place of care, not control.

Encourage others to prepare as well. The peace you experience in putting things in order will become a model for them. When one person in a family takes the brave step of planning intentionally, it often inspires others to do the same. You can become the example, the one who turned what could have been confusion into calm.

Leaving a legacy of peace is not only about ending well; it is about teaching those who follow how to live with intention and unity. It reminds everyone that love is most powerful when it is organized, communicated, and shared.

When your family can gather without conflict, knowing they are carrying out your wishes as you intended, you will have given them one of the greatest gifts possible: the peace of understanding, the ease of direction, and the healing that only clarity can bring.

Chapter 8 Reflection: Leaving a Legacy of Peace

1. What does "leaving a legacy of peace" mean to you personally? How would you like your family to feel after carrying out your wishes?

2. Are there unresolved tensions or misunderstandings in your family that you hope your planning will help ease? What steps can you take now to support healing?

3. What fears or concerns do you have about how your family might handle your final arrangements? How can you address them with clarity and compassion?

4. Which parts of your funeral plan might reduce stress, confusion, or conflict for your loved ones?

5. If your family has a history of disagreement or hierarchy, what can you do now to make your wishes unmistakably clear?

6. Have you witnessed conflict around funerals in the past? What did you learn from those experiences, and how does it shape what you want for your own farewell?

7. What message of unity, forgiveness, or compassion do you want your loved ones to carry after your transition?

8. What final instructions can you give that will help your family honor your plan without confusion or emotional burden?

CHAPTER 9

Your Homegoing Journal (Guided Prompts)

This section is where your reflections become the written plan. This is your space to write, to name, and to shape the story of how you want to be remembered. Think of it as a sacred conversation with yourself. This story becomes a gift to those who will one day read your words. There are no right or wrong answers here, only truth. Let these questions serve as prompts to guide your heart as you put your legacy into writing.

1. What three to four words describe the life you have lived?

Pause and reflect on the essence of your journey. Were you resilient, compassionate, joyful, disciplined, adventurous, or faithful? Think of the words that best capture how you moved through the world, how you loved, served, and grew.

2. Who should be part of your service, and why?

List the names of those who have shaped your story, your family, mentors, friends, or spiritual leaders. Consider who can speak, sing, or serve in a way that honors your spirit. Reflect on the tone you want the service to be calm and reverent, or filled with joy and testimony.

3. What scriptures, songs, or quotes capture your faith?

Write the verses or lyrics that ground you. Include the ones that have guided your life and lifted you in tough times. This may be a concise list of many choices. Perhaps:

- Psalm 23, "*The Lord is my shepherd . . .*"

- 2 Timothy 4:7, "*I have fought the good fight . . .*"

- A favorite hymn or gospel song that brings you peace. You might also include an ancestral proverb, quote, or poem that connects your faith to your heritage.

4. How would you like to be remembered?

Think beyond accomplishments. How do you want people to *feel* when they think of you? What values or examples do you hope they carry forward? Consider how you have shown love, courage, forgiveness, or grace, and how that legacy can live on in those who remain.

5. What message do you want to leave for your children or grandchildren?

This is your chance to speak directly to the next generation. What wisdom would you pass down if this were your final conversation? What blessing, warning, or prayer would you offer? You may write this as a letter, warm, simple, and full of love, so that your voice can still guide them long after your presence is gone.

Take your time with these pages. You may return to them often, adding or changing as your life evolves. The goal is not perfection; it is about presence. Each word you write becomes a part of your legacy of love; a piece of your story preserved for those who will carry it forward.

Chapter 9 Reflection: Your Homegoing Journal

1. What are the three words that best describe the life you have lived so far? Why do these words matter to you?

2. When you think about your homegoing, what is the emotion you want people to feel most strongly, joy, peace, gratitude, unity, love?

3. Which moments or accomplishments do you hope people will remember and celebrate?

4. What relationships have shaped your life the most, and how do you want them honored at your farewell?

5. What music speaks to your spirit?

6. What message do you want to leave for your children, grandchildren, or the next generation coming behind you?

7. What unfinished business, conversations, forgiveness, healing would you like to complete or begin before you transition?

8. If you could write one sentence that captures the legacy you want to leave, what would it be?

Sample Letters of Love to Leave Behind

As I promised, my desire is for you to move through this handbook with confidence, peace, and a steady heart. This reading and exercise are not meant to add anxiety or stress to your life. Instead, it is designed to help you with clarity, intention, and the joy of knowing your love will reach those you care about long after you are gone.

This handbook is, at its core, love expressed through preparation, thoughtfulness, and legacy. That is why, in this section, I invite you to take one gentler step: writing personal letters to the people who have shaped your life.

These are not meant to be heavy or overwhelming. In fact, I encourage you to think of these letters the same way you would think of a beautiful greeting card, or a handwritten note slipped into someone's hand at just the right moment: as expressions of appreciation. Words that warm the heart. Sentences that capture the essence of your relationship with the person you are writing to.

What would you want them to know?

What comfort would you want to offer?

What memory, blessing, or affirmation would you want them to carry forward?

To make this process easier and more meaningful, I have included sample letters for different people in your life: your spouse, your children, your sorority sisters, mentors, mentees, nieces, nephews, and friends. These examples are not meant to be copied word for word, but to serve as examples, helping you find your voice and set the tone for your own messages.

Let this be a joyful part of your journey. Consider it an extension of your gratitude, your legacy, and your heart. These letters are one more gift of love that will continue speaking long after your celebration of life is over. They can be as long or short as you wish. Allow your heart to open and your words to flow.

1. Letter to a Husband or Wife

My Beloved Spouse,

If you are reading this, I want you to feel my love surrounding you. You have been my companion, my partner, and the steady presence that made life's journey beautiful. Thank you for loving me fully not perfectly, but sincerely, faithfully, and deeply.

I want you to remember the best parts of what we shared. The laughter. The long talks. The quiet moments when simply being near you were enough. I am grateful for every season of our lives together, the triumphs we celebrated together and the challenges we stood firm through.

Please continue to live this joy. Rest well, eat well, travel, pray, laugh loudly with our family and friends. Do the things we always talked about. And most of all, be kind to yourself.

Let peace and God's love be your companion and your guide. My love does not end here; it simply changes form.

Forever yours,
Your Spouse (personalize)

2. Letter to Children

My Dear Children,

I want you to know that each of you has been a blessing beyond measure. Being your (mother/father) has been one of the greatest joys of my life. You made me proud in ways words will never fully express.

If grief feels heavy, let love carry you. Hold tightly to one another. Family is one of God's greatest gifts, and the bond you share will help you through every valley and every victory you encounter.

Remember the lessons I tried to live so that you could see, choose kindness, walk with integrity, pray without ceasing, and love bravely. Live your lives fully and enjoy the big and the small things, the loud and quiet things.

Celebrate your wins. Forgive quickly. Tell the truth. Keep going even when life feels hard. And when you think of me, let that memory lead you toward hope, not sorrow.

I will always be proud of you.

With all the love a heart can hold,
(mom/dad)

Legacy Letter to My Grandchildren

My Precious Grandchildren,

You are the special and exceptional love of my life. From the moment each of you entered this world, you added a new kind of joy to my heart, a joy I did not even know was possible. Grandchildren have a way of opening a soft, sacred space inside of us, and you have done exactly that for me.

I want you to know that being your (grandmother/grandfather) has been one of the greatest blessings God ever allowed me to experience. My love for you is deep, wide, and everlasting. Even if I could not be at every milestone, every game, school event, birthday, or celebration, please know that I carried you with me everywhere I went. My heart was always cheering for you, always praying for you, always believing in you.

The love between grandparents and grandchildren is unlike anything else. It is softer, wiser, and more patient. It sees you not only for who you are today, but for who you are becoming. It gives you room to grow, to explore, to make mistakes, and to rise again. And it wants nothing more than to see you live freely, joyfully, and boldly.

My hope for each of you is simple: that you live your life fully and beautifully. Be kind, be courageous, and be faithful. Trust God, chase your dreams, protect your peace, and hold onto family.

Whenever you think of me, I want you to smile. Remember the laughter, the stories, the hugs, the prayers, and the moments of joy and happiness we shared. Carry those memories as reminders that you were loved with a rare and unconditional love, the kind that only a grandparent can give.

I will always be proud of you. I will always be rooting for you. And I will always love you, beyond time and beyond measure.

With all my heart,
(Grandmother/grandfather)

3. Letter to Mentors

Dear (Mentor),

As I reflect on my journey, I cannot help but think of you. Thank you for speaking life into me when I needed it, for making space for my growth, and for modeling excellence and compassion in a way that shaped my path.

Your wisdom fortified me. Your honesty sharpened me. Your belief in me helped me believe in myself. I hope you know that the seeds you planted have produced a life of service, purpose, and gratitude.

Thank you for every lesson, every moment of correction, every affirmation, and every opportunity. My life is richer because you were part of it.

With deepest respect and appreciation,
(Mentee)

4. Letter to Mentees

Dear (Mentee),

Mentoring you has been one of the joys of my life. I loved watching you step into your purpose and your brilliance. You have everything you need to rise courage, faith, intelligence, compassion, and heart.

As you move forward, protect your integrity. Honor your gifts. Get rest, joy, and healing. And remember that leadership is not defined by titles or applause, but by service, humility, and resilience.

Keep learning. Keep stretching. Keep glowing. You are capable of extraordinary things. Wherever you go, take my belief in you with you.

I am proud of you, truly and deeply.

With love,
(Mentor)

5. Letter to Nieces and Nephews

Dear Nephews and Nieces,

You have brought delight and pride into my life. Even when I could not be there for every moment or milestone, I carried you in my heart.

My hope for you is simple: that you live fully and freely, with courage and joy. Stay connected to family. Honor where you come from. And chase the dreams that light up your soul.

You are part of my legacy, and I pray that your life will be marked by kindness, wisdom, and purpose. When you think of me, remember my love for you and let it lift your spirit.

Affectionately,
(Aunt/Uncle)

Longer General Legacy Letter

A letter that can be placed in the program or shared with all loved ones.

My Dear Family and Friends,

If you are reading this, then you are part of the circle of love that shaped my life. I want you to know what an honor it has been to walk this journey with you. My days were filled with meaning because of the relationships we nurtured, the lessons we shared, and the joy we found together.

Please do not let grief overshadow gratitude. Instead, let my memory bring you warmth. I hope you feel inspired to live fully, laugh often, forgive quickly, and love boldly. Life is shorter than we ever imagine, but it is also richer than we sometimes realize.

Know that I am grateful for every conversation, every prayer, every shared meal, every moment of laughter, and even the challenges that helped us grow. We were not perfect, but we were present for each other, and that is a blessing.

If there were times when I disappointed you, I ask your forgiveness. If there were times you disappointed me, I give forgiveness freely and completely. Let no unfinished conversation or unanswered question trouble your heart. Release it. Let love have the last word.

Remember the best of me; anything else should not matter now. I hope that my joy, my faith, my resilience, my love for beauty, and my commitment to service will be the lasting thoughts. And take good care of one another. Life is easier when you walk in unity.

May God's peace surround you now and always.

With eternal love and gratitude,
(your name here)

*What we place in God's hands today
becomes peace for our loved ones tomorrow.*

A CLOSING PRAYER

Dear God,

Thank You for the reader who now stands at the sacred threshold of preparation, not of fear, but of faith. Thank You for their courage to look ahead with peace, their willingness to write what love would want remembered.

Bless their hands as they begin this work. Let each word they write carry clarity, dignity, and the light of their spirit. Remind them that this is not about death, but about order, not about endings, but about legacy. May discipline meet inspiration, and seriousness be balanced by joy.

Give them enthusiasm for the task, knowing that in completing it, they are freeing their loved ones to grieve without confusion and to celebrate without burden. Surround them with the calm assurance that planning their homegoing is an act of selflessness, grace, and wisdom.

May they approach this sacred assignment with reverence and laughter, with a trusted friend who helps them keep the promise of completion. Let the month ahead be filled with small victories, pages written, memories recalled, peace unfolding.

And when they finish, let them feel a quiet joy rise within, the deep satisfaction of knowing they have lived and prepared with intention. Let their legacy be one of love, clarity, and calm, carried gently from their hands into the hearts of those who will follow.

Amen.

*Legacy is not measured by
what we leave behind, but by the peace
we leave within others.*

ACKNOWLEDGMENT

To those who continually encourage me, even when my plate is overflowing, thank you for recognizing how important writing is to me and to the lessons I am privileged to share.

My heartfelt thanks go first to my publisher, Willa Robinson, who has partnered with me time and again to bring my voice into the world. Thank you to Addis Huyler and Jason Rahming for the stunning photography and cover design that give this book great appeal.

Finally, I want to honor my brother Paul Ramon Parrish, who transitioned on June 1, 2024. Trusting me with his Five Wishes inspired me to put these very lessons into writing. His voice, care, and love are woven into every page.

With love and gratitude,

Barbara A. Perkins

Even in goodbye,
God offers comfort, order, and hope.

ABOUT THE AUTHOR

Dr. Barbara A. Perkins is an esteemed Executive Leadership Coach, author, and inspirational speaker dedicated to empowering individuals to achieve personal and professional growth. With over 25 years of experience in human and organizational development, Barbara has cultivated a unique approach to coaching that blends wisdom, compassion, and actionable strategies.

As the founder of Image Builders Etcetera, a leadership development and coaching firm, and Barbara A. Perkins Consultancy, LLC, she has worked with clients across various industries, guiding them to unlock their potential and foster high-performance teams. Barbara is committed to excellence and elevating those she is engaged. Through coaching and being on faculty at the Dorothy I. Height Global Leadership Academy, she desires to fill the pipeline with Black women ready to lead at home in the US and abroad.

An accomplished author of seven books on coaching, mentoring, and leadership, Barbara uses her writing to share insights and strategies that inspire others. Her deep faith and belief in the transformative power of joy underpins her coaching philosophy, encouraging clients to embrace their journeys with hope and purpose. When not coaching or writing, Barbara enjoys time with her family: her husband of 39 years, two adult children, and a six-year-old grandson.

For additional information about the author and her work, please visit
www.barbaraaperkinsconsultancy.com

DISCOVER MORE BOOKS BY DR. BARBARA A. PERKINS:

Coaching Yourself on Joy

Coaching Yourself on Betrayal

Coaching Yourself on Marriage

The Magic of Mentoring: Pearls of Wisdom

Coaching Yourself on Grief

Restoration: Seven Promises of God